# Civil Rights Pioneer

# Civil Rights Pioneer

## A Story about Mary Church Terrell

by Gwenyth Swain
illustrated by Ellen Beier

A Creative Minds Biography

Carolrhoda Books, Inc./Minneapolis

This book is available in two editions:
Library binding by Carolrhoda Books, Inc.,
    a division of Lerner Publishing Group
Soft cover by First Avenue Editions,
    an imprint of Lerner Publishing Group
241 First Avenue North, Minneapolis, MN 55401 U.S.A.

Website address: www.lernerbooks.com


Library of Congress Cataloging-in-Publication Data

Swain, Gwenyth.
    Civil rights pioneer : a story about Mary Church Terrell / by Gwenyth Swain ; illustrated by Ellen Beier.
        p.   cm.
    Includes bibliographical references and index.
    Summary: A biography of a determined woman, who was born in Tennessee, educated in Ohio, and lived in Washington, D.C., where she worked to gain equal rights for herself and other African Americans.
    ISBN: 1-57505-355-1 (lib. bdg. : alk. paper)
    ISBN: 0-8225-4170-X (pbk. : alk. paper)
    1. Terrell, Mary Church, 1863–1954—Juvenile literature. 2. Afro-American women civil rights workers—United States—Biography—Juvenile literature. 3. Afro-Americans—Biography—Juvenile literature. 4. Afro-Americans— Civil rights—Washington (D.C.)—History—20th century—Juvenile literature. 5. Washington (D.C.)—Biography—Juvenile literature.  [1. Terrell, Mary Church, 1863–1954. 2. Civil rights workers. 3. Afro-Americans—Biography. 4. Women—Biography.] I. Beier, Ellen, ill. II. Title.
E185.97.T47S93   1999
323'.092—dc21
[B]                                                                    98-28375

Manufactured in the United States of America
2 3 4 5 6 7 – MA – 08 07 06 05 04 03

# Table of Contents

# Introduction

Have you ever gotten into trouble when you knew you hadn't done anything wrong? That happened to Mollie Church, back in the 1860s, before she turned six years old. Mollie was on a train, sitting alone on a nice, soft seat by the window while her father smoked a cigar in the smoker car.

Mollie had been known to misbehave on trains (and in other places) before. Her favorite thing to do was to press her face against the window glass, her knees and feet up on the seat to boost her higher. But on this particular day, she was, as she later described, "sitting up 'straight and proper.'" Not only that, but for once, she boasted, ". . . My hands were clean and so was my face. I hadn't mussed my hair; it was brushed back and was perfectly smooth. I hadn't lost either one of the two pieces of blue ribbon which tied the little braids on each side of my head."

7

That was why Mollie was so shocked and scared when the white man in the conductor's uniform grabbed her by the shoulders and yelled, "Whose little nigger is this?"

Mollie wasn't sure what the word *nigger* meant, but the man made it sound so bad she froze. She certainly was glad when one of her father's white friends went to find him in the smoker car. Robert Church was so light skinned, he could pass for white. He also carried a gun with him, for safety, at all times. One thing or the other persuaded the conductor to stop bothering Mollie. She was confused but relieved.

During the rest of the trip home, while she dried her tears, she thought about what had happened. No matter how she looked at it, she couldn't figure out how she'd misbehaved.

Later, Mollie asked her mother if she knew why the man on the train had been so mean. Mollie's mother gave her an answer, but it didn't make much sense. Sometimes, she explained, holding Mollie close, even when we are very good, people are angry and mean.

# 1

# Mollie Church

Despite that bad time on the train, most of Mollie Church's early memories were of good times. She was born Mary Eliza Church on September 23, 1863, in the Southern city of Memphis, Tennessee. Mary, or Mollie as everyone called her, was born during the Civil War.

At that time, Southern states disagreed with Northern states over many things, including whether or not white people should be able to buy and sell and own black people as their slaves. The South was fighting the North partly to protect the right of whites to own slaves.

By the time Mollie was old enough to remember much, the war was over. The South had lost its battle, and all the slaves were free. Even though Mollie's mother, Louisa, and her father, Robert, had been born slaves, they rarely talked about it. Both had been given their freedom early, before the war. Once in a while, Mrs. Church would show Mollie some of the clothes her master's daughter, Miss Laura, had bought for her in New York City, before Mollie's mother had gotten her freedom and married Bob Church. Mrs. Church told Mollie that Miss Laura and her father were kind, but she never told her daughter what it felt like to be someone's slave.

Only Mollie's grandmother—Louisa Church's mother—talked about old times. Aunt Liza, as everyone called her, was a large and loving black woman. While Mollie sat in her grandmother's ample lap, Aunt Liza told her stories of slave days.

Aunt Liza's stories were upsetting—and thrilling. There were tales about being poor—so poor she'd had to sleep on the floor, instead of a bed. There were scary stories, like the one about a snake that would chase bad children in the woods around the plantation.

11

Then there was the story about the time the overseer came after Aunt Liza with his whip. The overseer was the man who made sure the slaves did what they were supposed to do. He turned up in many of Aunt Liza's stories; sometimes he reminded Mollie of the train conductor. But when Mollie tried to comfort her grandmother, Aunt Liza would always just laugh and say, "Never mind, honey. . . . Gramma ain't a slave no more."

Aunt Liza, Mollie decided later, was right to laugh. The Churches weren't slaves, they didn't have to worry about the overseer anymore, and they certainly weren't poor. Mollie lived with her parents and Aunt Liza in a big two-story house on South Lauderdale Street in Memphis. In 1867, when Mollie was four, her brother, Thomas, was born. Even with all that family, the house wasn't crowded. Upstairs, there were several bedrooms, plus screened-in porches for sleeping on hot, muggy summer nights. Downstairs, Mollie was supposed to stay out of the "company" rooms—the parlor and the dining room. In back, over the carriage house, there were rooms for the Churches' cook and other servants.

With money she'd earned styling hair at her very own beauty salon, Mollie's mother had bought the family its first buggy and the house on South

Lauderdale. Day and night, Mrs. Church was busy at her salon near Court Square, in downtown Memphis's best shopping area. Most of the customers were wealthy white women, and they relied on Lou Church to give them the latest look.

Mollie's father had had his share of success as well. Before the Civil War, he had worked his way up from cabin boy to ship's steward, working on steamboats that traveled up and down the Mississippi River. When the war ended and steamboat traffic dried to a trickle, Bob Church found work on land. He ran a bar in Memphis, but he wasn't quite as successful as his wife.

On Sundays, Bob Church took Mollie to visit his old boss on the steamboat, Captain C. B. Church. Mollie looked forward to the weekly visits. She usually got an orange to keep and a friendly pat on the head. The captain and Mollie's father would talk while Mollie tried to sit still and behave. Captain Church's house was grand, one of the biggest houses in one of the wealthiest white neighborhoods in Memphis. Mollie thought it was nice of the captain to let them visit each week.

"Captain Church is certainly good to us, Papa," Mollie remarked one Sunday as the two of them left the house. She held the fruit and flowers Captain

Church had sent home with her. "And don't you know, Papa," Mollie continued, "you look just like Captain Church."

Mollie stopped suddenly. She hadn't realized what she was saying until she'd said it: Nice old Captain Church looked like her own father for a reason. The captain was her papa's father—no doubt about it. Captain Church must also be her grandfather.

The more Mollie thought about it, the more sense it made. It explained why their last names were the same. And it explained why the captain treated Mollie and her papa so well. (No other white man in Memphis invited them into his home as the captain did.) There were a few things, however, that Mollie couldn't explain. Why, if Captain Church was her grandfather, did she and her father always enter the captain's house by the back door? And why did Bob Church never call the captain Papa?

When she was older, Mollie came to understand that Captain Church was kinder to them than most white men would have been in those days. He had given his son the Church family name and his freedom, long before slavery was outlawed. He had also given Mollie's father a good job on his steamboat. And when young Bob Church showed his abilities, Captain Church made sure he was promoted.

15

But when Mollie was young, she didn't understand all this. She only knew that she had a white granddaddy who, unlike Aunt Liza, would never hold her on his knee and tell her stories of the old days back before the war that ended slavery.

Was Captain Church upset with her? Mollie wondered. Was that why he didn't call her his grandbaby?

On her next visit to the captain's house, Mollie tried to be quieter and better behaved than ever. But before she could see if her plan was working, her life got turned upside down.

Six-year-old Mollie wasn't sure what she had done to cause the trouble this time—or even if she had caused the trouble at all. But she was certain that things were changing at home, and changing for the worse. Mollie's parents weren't talking to each other anymore, only yelling. Both of them looked angry and tired and sad. Mollie would have done anything to make things better, but she didn't have a chance.

Robert and Louisa Church had decided to separate. Four-year-old Thomas stayed with his father. Mollie moved with her mother to a new home just a few blocks from the salon on Court Street. The lawyers and Mollie's parents and a judge argued in court over the family's future. Her father, Mollie learned, was trying to persuade the judge to let Thomas continue living with him.  But when Mollie's parents were finally divorced, the judge gave custody of both Mollie and Thomas to their mother.

# 2

# Boiling Her Peas

That September, Mollie Church turned seven and her whole world changed at once. Mollie hadn't even had a chance to get used to the idea of living away from her father when she was put on a train headed north. Her parents had decided it would be best if Mollie went away to school in Ohio. During the train ride, Mollie sat as quietly as possible while her mother tried to explain.

Mollie could learn so much more at a Northern school, Lou Church said. In the South, schools were segregated. There were separate schools for white children and black children, and the schools for black children were hardly schools at all. Mollie had learned her ABCs in a makeshift classroom in a Memphis church basement. Bob and Lou Church agreed that their daughter deserved better. The Model School in Yellow Springs, Ohio, was just the ticket.

Once in Yellow Springs, Mrs. Church gave Mollie a good-bye hug and left her to board with a prominent African American family, the Hunsters. "Ma" Hunster ran the Union House Hotel, while "Pa" Hunster was in charge of the best ice-cream parlor for miles around. The Hunsters treated Mollie like family, and she grew fond of them all. She especially liked Miss Sallie, one of the two grown-up Hunster daughters. One of the Hunsters' grown sons lived with them and had a small candy store on the ground floor of their large, comfortable home. (With her allowance of five dollars each month—a huge sum for a little girl in the 1870s—Mollie was a frequent customer at both the ice-cream parlor and the sweetshop.)

To anyone who looked in on Mollie during her years in Yellow Springs, it would have seemed as if she adjusted to her new life with no effort at all. She studied hard and always did well enough to stay at the head of her class. She even seemed to fit right into her new home.

Still, something was missing. Mollie's candy allowance, sent by her father each month, was the envy of her classmates. But Mollie would have given it up in a minute to see her papa just once. Her mother's Christmas boxes were filled with wonders—beautiful dolls, golden rings, fashionable hats, and other delights for Mollie, along with dresses for Miss Sallie and her sister and gifts for all the other Hunsters. But once the wrappings were burned and the presents were put away, Mollie still longed to see her mother again.

Perhaps because of the trouble she thought she had caused in the past, Mollie made a special effort to get along with people in Yellow Springs and later in Oberlin. That was where her parents sent her in 1875 to attend high school.

Oberlin, Ohio, was in the flat northern part of the state, not far from Lake Erie. Mollie missed the hills and valleys around Yellow Springs and the warmth of the Hunster family. In Oberlin, she stayed in a boardinghouse. When she entered the eighth grade at the public high school, she discovered she was the only black student in her class.

Rather than feeling lonely or sorry for herself, Mollie again made the best of things. At the boardinghouse, she found that when she put her mind to it, she could get along with a houseful of strangers.

At school, she discovered that being an "only" wasn't all bad—in fact, being the only black girl in her class sometimes made her feel special.

By the time she graduated from high school in 1879, Mollie Church had given her brand of making the best of things a name, "boiling peas." She talked about her philosophy in the speech she gave at graduation.

There was a story, she explained to the audience, about two monks. Both were told to put peas in their shoes and walk to the next town. Since these were hard, dried peas, it would not be a comfortable walk. But when the men arrived in the next town, one monk was in pain and the other wasn't. The suffering monk asked the other for his secret, and the other replied that he had taken the time to boil his peas.

To Mollie, boiling her peas meant working hard to make others respect and accept her. It meant accepting things she couldn't change, yet trying in small ways to make them better.

Giving a speech in front of so many people was exciting for Mollie, but the best part was knowing that her mother was in the audience. Lou Church had traveled all the way from her new home in New York City to see Mollie graduate. After her mother returned home, Mollie would be spending the entire summer vacation with her father back in Memphis.

Mollie's long-awaited reunion with her papa was all too short. In the summer of 1879, a deadly yellow fever epidemic swept through Memphis and much of the South. Thousands of people were dying, and doctors had no cure.

Hoping to put his daughter beyond reach of the epidemic, Bob Church sent Mollie home to Oberlin, taking her as far as Cincinnati himself. Then he turned back. Mollie's father was making a shrewd but dangerous gamble. Betting that he wouldn't become sick, he returned to Memphis and bought houses and other property. With so many dead and dying from yellow fever, people who weren't sick were leaving town. They sold their property at low prices, partly because they believed Memphis would never be safe to live in again. If Bob Church survived the epidemic—and if people moved back to Memphis—he stood to become a very rich man.

When his gamble paid off, Mollie's father became the South's first black millionaire. His good fortune helped give Mollie courage when she needed to ask him for a big favor. She wanted more money for her education.

After Mollie had graduated from high school, her parents had agreed that she should go on to college. In the 1870s, it was unusual for a young woman—

black or white—to go to college. But Mollie, or Mary as she had started to call herself, was an unusual person. Oberlin, too, was an unusual town. Along with a public high school that welcomed students of all colors, Oberlin was home to the first college in the United States to admit black students.

Mary's parents had planned for her to attend Oberlin College and take the two-year "ladies' course." Mary had happily agreed to study at Oberlin, but she wanted to take the longer and costlier "gentlemen's course." If she took the two-year course, she wouldn't get a college diploma, only a certificate. As far as Mary knew, there were less than a handful of black women with college degrees in the country. She wanted to be part of that handful—even if it meant trying to convince Bob Church to spend money on something most people would think silly and unnecessary.

Mary's father didn't take much convincing after all. He was glad to do what he could to make his daughter happy. Mary found it harder to convince some of her friends. How was Mary ever going to find someone to marry if she took the gentlemen's course? they asked. Finding a black man who knew Latin and Greek—two things Mary would be studying in college—was, they said, "like hunting for a needle in a haystack." And how was she ever going to find time for parties and dances if she was taking classes in algebra and geometry?

Mary had answers for most of her friends' questions. She would have plenty of time for dances and parties later. They thought Greek was stuffy and boring, but Mary had taken some classes in it already and she liked it. Mary did wonder if her friends were right on one point. Would she ever find a husband—a husband who knew just as much Greek and Latin as she did? It was a long shot, but Mary decided to take her chances.

When Mary graduated from Oberlin College in 1884, she was probably one of the ten best-educated black women in the United States. Mary felt keenly how lucky she was. That was why she felt such disappointment when she realized what kind of life her father meant for her after college.

Mary hoped to use her education to help other black people. Mr. Church wanted his daughter to be the hostess at his new home in Memphis. Mary's father had sent her blueprints of the mansion while it was still in the planning stages. The size and beauty of the place still took Mary by surprise. Bob Church was wealthy, and he intended to live as other wealthy Southerners did. So far as he knew, no young Southern belles worked—they threw dinner parties and waited to marry Southern gentlemen.

Mary tried to be a good hostess, but her heart wasn't in it. When her father announced his plans to marry Miss Anna Wright, Mary was almost relieved. Her father seemed truly happy with his fiancée, and Mary wished them well. But Bob Church's marriage to Anna Wright ended forever one secret hope of Mary's. For years, she had imagined that if she were the best daughter possible, her parents might get back together again.

With that dream gone, Mary set her sights on a new dream: getting a job. In 1885 Mary accepted a teaching position at Wilberforce University in Ohio. She loved grading papers, preparing lectures, and playing the organ at church services on campus. But just two years later, Mary was ready to move on. She had heard about an even better job in Washington, D.C.

In the late 1800s, the nation's capital seemed to be the place where all the most interesting and intellectual African Americans gathered. Mary had already visited Washington once before in 1881. Some of her father's friends had invited her to President James Garfield's inaugural ball. To Mary, the District of Columbia had lived up to its nickname, "The Negroes Paradise."

In Washington, she had danced in the same room as the president and had been the guest of a senator and his wife. She had even had the privilege of meeting Frederick Douglass, who was the most famous and powerful black man of his day. Like Mary's parents, Douglass had been born a slave. When Mary met him, Douglass was serving as United States marshal for the District of Columbia. Douglass had been at the president's inauguration, too—he stood beside Garfield when the new president took the oath of office.

Washington's M Street High School was one of the best high schools in the country for black students, and Mary was applying for a job in the school's Latin department. The man Mary would be working for sounded even more impressive than the school. Even before she arrived for her interview, Mary had heard about Robert Heberton Terrell. Terrell had graduated from Washington's black public schools and was among the first African Americans to be admitted to Harvard. Mary had heard that he was handsome and unmarried. She was already counting on the fact that he knew Greek as well as Latin.

# 3

# Travels and Trials

When Mary saw what one of her students had written on the chalkboard, she had to cover her smile. Before she washed it off, she reread the message. "Mr. Terrell is certainly getting good," it said. "He used to go to dances, but now he goes to Church."

Whoever wrote it was right. Mr. Terrell and his assistant, Miss Church, got along very well. Everyone who knew them seemed to have been expecting the two to marry—almost from the day they met.

It didn't take Mary long to realize that she was very fond of Robert Terrell. At the same time, she was fond of her new job, and Mary knew that married women were not allowed to teach. In the late 1800s, a married woman was expected to raise babies, not teach Latin. Teaching was too exciting to give up, especially when she'd only just started. At twenty-three, Mary had many dreams for the future, and they didn't all include a husband.

One dream became a reality sooner than she expected. Mary's father wanted to send her to Europe. At that time, a white American graduating from college wasn't considered truly well educated without studying and traveling in the great cities of Europe. Bob Church was offering Mary the same opportunity, and she couldn't pass it up.

By the summer of 1888, Mary and her father were steaming across the Atlantic Ocean on the *City of Berlin*. After traveling together in France that summer, Mr. Church returned to Memphis and Mary settled in Lausanne, Switzerland. There she polished her French by speaking it with people who didn't understand English.

After a year, Mary spoke French well enough to be ready for a new challenge. She moved to Berlin, where she worked on improving her German. By the time she returned to her teaching job at the M Street School in 1890, Mary's studies in Europe had earned her a master's degree in languages. With her new degree, Mary Church was probably the best-educated black woman in the country.

That's why some people were surprised when she gave up her high school teaching job and turned down an even better job at Oberlin in order to marry Robert Terrell in 1891. It wasn't an easy decision for Mary. Afterward, she would always explain it by saying, "I enjoyed assisting him in the Latin department so much, I made up my mind to assist him in all departments for the rest of my natural life."

The marriage of Mary Eliza Church and Robert Heberton Terrell was reported in black newspapers across the country. Bob Church paid for the wedding and Mary's wardrobe. Everything at the wedding and the banquet would have been perfect, but one person was missing. Mary's parents still didn't want to be in the same place at the same time. Lou Church helped Mary choose her clothes and flowers, but she didn't come to the wedding. While Mary was being married in Memphis, her mother stood alone in her New York apartment. Lou Church made a point of wearing the very same dress and hat she would have worn to the wedding.

As soon as the Terrells moved into their apartment in the Anacostia neighborhood of Washington, D.C., Mary set out to prove that a college-educated woman could be a good housekeeper. In the late 1800s, many people—men and women alike—thought that too much education would spoil a woman for housework. Some people even suggested that too much college might make a woman sick or insane.

Mary wasn't worried about such strange views. She just wanted to prove she could boil eggs as well as the next person. For a time, Mary was content to do all the things people expected of a young married woman.

There was one part of the first years of her marriage, however, that left Mary sad and angry and confused. Mary and Robert lost too many babies. One baby was stillborn. A second baby died almost as soon as it was born. Then, in 1895, Mary's too-small baby boy died when he was only two days old. The boy had been put in a makeshift incubator; Washington's black hospital couldn't afford a real one. Mary knew the doctors had done everything they could. In a segregated society, their hospital and their equipment would always be second best. Mary believed her boy would have lived if he had been born in a hospital for whites.

After her baby's death, Mary's thoughts were some-times confused, but they always came back to the death of her childhood friend, Tom Moss. Just that spring, Mary had learned that Tom had been lynched by whites in Memphis. Rumor had it, Tom had been murdered for "succeeding too well." His business was doing better than the white-owned businesses on his street.

What chance would her little boy have had in such a world? Was it better that he had died? Mary's eyes filled with tears as she gazed at the silver oyster forks Tom Moss had given her as a wedding gift. But no matter how long or how hard Mary looked, Tom's gift and his short life gave no answers.

# 4

# Brothers, Sisters, and Daughters

Mary didn't lose her sadness altogether, but she did find ways to ease the pain. If she couldn't have children of her own, she was determined to shower her love and concern on other people. While she mourned the deaths of her babies, Mary looked around for ways to create a different kind of family.

In 1895 she was offered a position on the Washington, D.C., Board of Education. Here was a job that fit Mary perfectly, with her experience as a teacher and her ability to gently persuade others. Before long, she had persuaded the mostly white board members to agree to her plan to celebrate Douglass Day (in honor of Frederick Douglass) every February 14. Douglass Day would be celebrated only in schools for black students. Mary would rather have had all students in the District—black and white—honor Douglass. But when February 14 rolled around, she considered the celebration a victory.

Mary's work on the board of education gave her the chance to support blacks in the local schools. But soon she was looking for ways to carry her concerns beyond the District. Encouraged by her husband, Mary took to the lecture circuit. Beginning in the 1890s, she gave speeches in cities and towns across the country.

Often, when she lectured in the South, Mary was forced to sit in the drafty and dirty Jim Crow car of the train, the car reserved for black passengers. Mary wanted to tell the conductor that she and the others in the Jim Crow car deserved as good a seat as white passengers got, but she held her tongue. Partly it was the old fear. But mostly Mary saved her arguments for meeting halls and church pulpits, not trains.

When she lectured to groups of whites, Mary argued that black people deserved respect. White audiences, Mary was certain, had heard more lies than truths about African Americans. White-owned newspapers, particularly in the South, claimed that black people lived by lying and stealing and worse. Mary aimed to tell white Americans how black Americans really lived. Through her polished speeches, Mary also hoped white people would stop seeing just the color of her skin and start seeing her.

When she stood in the pulpits of Southern black churches on hot summer evenings, Mary shared all she knew about African Americans in the past and their great achievements. If she could tell everyone about the history of her people, Mary felt sure that black men, women, and children would go on to achieve more great things in the future.

The board of education and the lecture circuit were good places to start. But if Mary wanted all African Americans to feel the confidence they needed to achieve, she couldn't do it alone. When she joined the Colored Women's League of Washington, Mary knew she had found just the group to help her. The Colored Women's League was a group of well-educated, middle-class black women. They wanted to share some of the things they had learned in high school and college with black women who hadn't had the same opportunities.

Soon after she joined the League, Mary volunteered to teach English literature and German several nights a week. Although she was glad to be teaching again, Mary wondered if the women in her classes needed something more basic than German conversation lessons and the novels of Jane Austen.

When another, larger black women's organization, the Federation of Afro-American Women, asked to join with the League, Mary thought the two groups might look for more practical ways to serve black women. And when the two groups—together called the National Association of Colored Women—voted to have Mary as their president, she jumped at the chance.

When Mary Church Terrell spoke before the members of the NACW in 1896, she hoped people outside the room were listening. No longer would African American women be invisible, Mary said. With the leadership of the NACW, they would build kindergartens for black children. They would help working black women by providing child care in a network of day nurseries. They would set up rooming houses for young black working girls who couldn't get a room at the local YWCA. And they would bring modern ideas about good nutrition and good health to black women across the country through clubs for young mothers.

"In myself I am nothing," Mary told her sisters in the NACW, "but with the loyal support of conscientious, capable women, all things are possible. . . ." Mary could never have dreamed of trying to do all of these things on her own. But when she joined with other black women like herself, she felt freer to dream and to do.

Over the next few years, Mary and the NACW formed chapters across the country. With churches and other local groups, they found money to start dozens of kindergartens and nurseries. In Illinois, black women founded the Phyllis Wheatley Home for Girls. The home was named after the African-born American poet, known as Phillis Wheatley, and was devoted to helping working girls. The NACW also encouraged educated black women to volunteer to teach—both classes in literature and classes in more practical skills.

Mary's work with the NACW left her feeling fired up with enthusiasm. She only wished she had more time to give to it, but she had a growing family to care for. In 1898 Mary had found out she was pregnant again, and she insisted on going to New York—and a better hospital—for the birth of this child.

The healthy baby girl, Phyllis, made Mary happier than she had ever been before. Not long after Phyllis was born, Mary's brother, Thomas, asked the Terrells to adopt his young daughter, also named Mary. To make the family complete (and to make the Terrells' home even more snug), Mary's mother moved in.

Lou Church was retired and looked forward to helping out with her granddaughters while Mary was away at lectures and meetings. Most important of all, she was looking forward to spending some time with her daughter. Once Lou Church settled in, she and Mary set about trying "to make up for lost time." Mary hadn't realized before how lonely she had been for a mother—and how lonely Lou had been for a daughter—during Mary's years in Ohio. At last the family felt complete.

With a bigger family to support, Robert Terrell was pleased to be earning more money in a job that also earned him much respect. While Mary had been lecturing and organizing women, Robert had earned a law degree at Howard University. In 1901 he was offered a job as a federal judge in the District of Columbia.

The president of the United States appointed federal judges, and Robert was the first African American to get such an important job. It didn't come without strings attached, however. Every four years, the president had to reappoint Robert Terrell to his job. And every four years, the all-white United States Senate voted on whether or not to confirm Judge Terrell's appointment. Many Southern senators hated the idea of giving a prestigious job to a black man. Mary knew they would take any excuse to appoint a white man instead. She worried that anything she said or did might hurt her husband's chances of keeping his job. If the situation frustrated her, Mary didn't let it show. Instead, she boiled her peas and turned her attention to her family.

Even with her mother's help, Mary hadn't found much time for work outside her home. After several terms as president of the NACW, Mary left the group in 1901. She lectured less often and closer to home. And in 1911, she ended her years of service on the board of education.

These days when she wanted to get a point across and help African Americans, Mary turned to pen and paper. She found time to write a few pages at night after the girls were in bed or while watching over a sick child. At first, Mary tried writing made-up stories, but she had better luck writing about the real world.

In 1907, when Mary was over forty years old, one of her articles was published in a well-known magazine, *The Independent.* In "What It Means To Be Colored in the Capital of the United States," Mary told the true story of life in the District. She still remembered the freedom she had felt when she'd attended President Garfield's inaugural ball. But over twenty years had passed. Times had changed.

As the wife of a judge, Mary lived a privileged life. But she, too, had felt the frustration of not being able to get a good job, or a meal in a restaurant, or a room in a hotel in the nation's capital because she was black.  Recently, Mary had tried to buy a cup of coffee at her favorite drugstore counter at the corner of F and Ninth Streets.  Mary went there so often, her face was familiar.  That didn't stop the waitress from telling her that black people weren't being served there anymore.  In her article, Mary tried not to cause offense, but her words were strong.

Black friends talked to Mary about her story and shared tales of their own experiences living in the District.  Mary was thrilled by the response, but sometimes she wondered what good words alone would do.  The situation in Washington, D.C., only seemed to grow worse, no matter how many articles she wrote.  Sometimes Mary was so busy with her children and so concerned about her husband's job that she didn't see how she was ever going to find the time or the opportunity to do more.  But remembering the humiliation she'd felt at that drugstore, Mary vowed someday, somehow to find the time.

# 5

# Lunch in the Nation's Capital

It took Mary Terrell longer than she expected to find the time to change things. Years passed. Her parents died. Her daughters went off to school, to work, and to married life. And finally, in 1920, Robert Terrell had a stroke. Mary helped Robert struggle along until December of 1925. Mary was sixty-two years old; Robert had just turned sixty-eight. When Robert died, all the trees in the District were bare of leaves. Winter was in the air. Mary felt as empty as the rooms in their big, new house on S Street.

Before long, however, she had picked up a pen again. She was ready to write the story of her life. Mary meant for her autobiography to be a great book, a best-seller that would make all Americans think about race. She spent nearly ten years writing and rewriting, polishing and revising.

When it was finally published, the book, called *A Colored Woman in a White World,* sold respectably and got good reviews. But some of the reviews surprised Mary. The way people talked, it was as if they thought she'd already died, gone to heaven, and been turned into a statue.

Being treated with respect was fine, but Mary did not like the sense that the world was ready to go on without her. She wasn't dead yet. If she had accomplished many things, that was all the more reason not to rest on her laurels.

Mary's neighbor Tomlinson Todd agreed. In the late 1940s, Mary Church Terrell looked like a small, sweet, and slightly frail grandmother of eighty-odd years. But Tommy Todd knew better. If anyone in the District could get things done, Mary Terrell could. That's why Mr. Todd started asking her what she was going to do about the old laws.

Todd and many other African Americans were talking about two recently rediscovered laws. The laws had been passed in 1872 and 1873—not long before Mary's first visit to the District. In those days, a black person could stay at a Washington hotel and eat at any restaurant in the District. Laws helped make that possible. The laws of 1872 and 1873 required "all eating-place proprietors to serve any respectable well-behaved person regardless of color, or face a $100 fine and forfeiture of their license for one year."

Any African American who had tried to eat a meal in a downtown Washington restaurant in the 1940s knew nobody was paying attention to the old laws. Yet a group of lawyers had recently said that, so far as they could tell, the laws had never been repealed. Years had passed and new law books had been printed. The laws of 1872 and 1873 had simply been left out of the books.

Mary Terrell knew quite a bit about laws, being the wife of a judge. So she was well aware that the District of Columbia's history was like a crazy quilt. The U.S. Congress was in charge of overseeing the District, and Congress seemed to try out a new form of government every few years. Laws passed in the 1870s had been made when the government of Washington, D.C., was very different from the way it was in the late 1940s. The people in charge of the District, the District commissioners, weren't sure the old laws were still good.

The more Mary Terrell read about the old laws, the more convinced she was that they were valid and should never be left out of a law book again. Mary could still feel the sting of the last time she had tried to get a cup of coffee downtown. It had happened over forty years before, but Mary thought about it every time she walked by that drugstore.

By 1950 Mary had a plan. The front room of her house on S Street was filled with people who, like Mary, wanted to eat where they pleased in the nation's capital. Mary, the Reverend William Jernagin, pastor of the Mount Carmel Baptist Church, and other volunteers formed a committee.

The Coordinating Committee for the Enforcement of the District of Columbia Anti-Discrimination Laws had a long name but a short list of goals. Volunteers would go around to eating places throughout the District to find out whether black people were being served. If a restaurant wasn't serving African Americans, then the committee would work to change the restaurant owner's mind. The committee also planned to go to court to prove once and for all that the laws of 1872 and 1873 were still valid.

The District commissioners had decided that the laws might still be good; they even said as much in February of 1950. But they also said they didn't want to enforce the laws until the courts had agreed. To get the courts' opinion, somebody would have to test the law. That was why Mary Terrell walked into Thompson's Restaurant on February 28. Thompson's was a restaurant chain. The company employed many black people, but blacks weren't served in the chain's cafeteria-style restaurants.

Mary, the Reverend Arthur Elmes, and Miss Essie Thompson were joined by a white friend, David Scull. Dressed in their Sunday best, the four walked together through the cafeteria line. The Reverend Elmes and Miss Thompson took a doughnut and a piece of pie from the counter. Mary Terrell asked for some soup. Mary took the steaming bowl from the server's hands and set it on her tray. She moved on down the line.

Before the group could pay for their food and be seated, the manager of Thompson's stopped them. Mr. Scull, he said, was welcome to eat at the restaurant. The others were not. Mary and her friends didn't argue just then. Instead, they headed to the District commissioners' office and filed a complaint.

Mary had never been in such an odd position in all her life. Here she was, the wife of a judge, and she was *trying* to end up in court. She had gone out of her way to make trouble—even if it was just by ordering a bowl of soup—and she wasn't at all sure things would turn out well. She hoped the courts could agree that the old laws were still good. But even good laws could be ignored. And many innocent people, including Mary's old friend Tom Moss back in Memphis, had been killed for doing things that didn't seem any more outlandish than ordering a bowl of soup.

When the case finally got a hearing in March, Mary and the others were encouraged. The local court judge seemed to be listening to their arguments. But in his decision that summer, the judge said that since the laws had been off the books for so long, they were no longer any good.

It was a typical Washington summer—hot, humid, and sticky—but Mary still found the energy to fight back. The committee started an appeal, the long process of asking a higher court to go over the local judge's decision. Mary hoped the committee would win the appeal. In the meantime, she and a group of volunteers set about meeting the committee's other goals.

Volunteers had spent months finding out where blacks could and could not get service in the eating places of Washington. They had discovered that local department stores and dime stores were some of the worst offenders. Stores like Kresge's, Hecht's, and Murphy's were glad to take money from black shoppers (so long as they didn't ask to try on clothing and so long as they let white customers pay first). Those same black shoppers, however, weren't allowed to eat at the stores' lunch counters. Why was her money good in one part of a store but not in another? Mary aimed to find out.

Committee members first tried negotiating with store owners. If friendly persuasion didn't work, the group then asked African Americans and sympathetic white people to stop shopping at the store. This tactic, called a boycott, hadn't been used much before. Some store owners found that it wasn't worth losing money; they started serving all shoppers.

If a store still wasn't convinced, the committee tried another tactic. Volunteers started spending Thursday evenings (when stores stayed open late) and weekends marching and carrying signs in front of racist five-and-dimes. Mary Church Terrell was in the first picket line when it formed outside Kresge's Department Store in December 1950. She and the others were warmly dressed and polite. They were mostly silent, but their signs spoke loudly. "GIVE THE GIFT OF DEMOCRACY TO WASHINGTON FOR CHRISTMAS," one sign read. "Don't buy at KRESGE'S."

Picketing at Kresge's was short and sweet. After just six weeks, Mary's group had persuaded Kresge's to serve all people at its lunch counters.

More good news followed. In May 1951, the case against Thompson's Restaurant was heard again. This time, the judge agreed with Mary and the others. The old laws were still good! Mary was on top of the world, but only for a moment. Thompson's appealed the judge's decision. And the District decided not to enforce the old laws while the case was working its way through the courts.

Mary poured all her energies into another picket, this time of Hecht's Department Stores. She was hoping for a quick victory to raise everyone's spirits.

She and others hoisted up signs reading:

DON'T BUY AT HECHT'S
HECHT'S JIM-CROW LUNCH COUNTER
DISGRACES THE NATION'S CAPITAL

HUMAN DIGNITY ISN'T WORTH A DIME
AT THIS DIME STORE

STAY OUT
SEGREGATION PRACTICED HERE

Hecht's didn't seem to mind. The pickets went on and on. In the summer's heat, Mary carried on the fight, but she paused from time to time to sit in a lawn chair next to the picket line. When winter came, she wore a heavy coat, strong boots, black gloves, and a proper black hat crowned with feathers. At home, she could warm up again, but she didn't get the rest she needed.

People called Mary on the phone at all hours. They threatened to hurt her and the other picketers. One person wrote to Mary, "Forcing yourself on white people won't change you any. You will still always be just a negro woman and don't forget that. . . . I don't want any part of Negroes, good ones or bad ones, and the only ones I have met are all bad."

It bothered Mary to be hated. Still, her goal wasn't to be liked; she wanted respect. Finally, in January 1952, Hecht's decided to honor the laws of 1872 and 1873 and serve "any respectable well-behaved person regardless of color."

Mary and the other members of the committee were thrilled. They were even happier when, by negotiating, boycotting, and picketing, they managed to change policies at all downtown dime stores over the next several months. But the committee also received some bad news.

The case against Thompson's Restaurants had gone to a higher court. There, the judge had agreed with Thompson's. Mary's group had lost again, and this time there was only one chance left.

The United States Supreme Court is the nation's highest court. Hours before the case was heard there, in late April 1953, a long line of people snaked down the sidewalk. There were only fifty-four seats in the courtroom, and many people wanted to be there to hear the case. They wanted to see history being made. Mary Terrell was sure to have a seat inside. She was eighty-nine years old and a respected elder in Washington's black community. People in the crowd made way for the straight-backed, smiling woman.

The members of the Supreme Court took only two days to hear the arguments for and against the old laws, but they spent many months considering them. When they made their decision on June 8, 1953, it was clear there would be no appeal. All members agreed that "the Acts of 1872 and 1873 survived . . . and remain today a part of the governing body of laws applicable to the District."

Mary was elated by the victory. But she didn't crow or brag. She urged people to get right back to work. If they wanted to be sure the laws would never be lost again, they had better go out for lunch—anywhere and everywhere in the District, Mary said. And they should think of their big win as a first step. It was everyone's duty, Mary said, to go right on "helping to break down barriers that keep our Washington from truly being the capital of the greatest democracy on earth, in which there is equal justice for all under the law."

Back when she wasn't quite six years old, sitting on a train and wondering at the conductor's anger, little

Mollie Church had worried about all the trouble she'd caused. She had tried to do her best in her younger days to "boil her peas" and get along without making waves. Bringing full democracy to the nation's capital would no doubt involve more boycotts and more pickets. But even if it meant causing some trouble and making a few waves, Mary Church Terrell was ready to lead the way.

# Afterword

Mary didn't have the chance to meet all her goals. She died while staying at her summer home near Annapolis, Maryland, on July 24, 1954. She was ninety years old.

Just a few months before Mary Terrell's death, the United States Supreme Court heard another important case. Mary hadn't been involved in *Brown versus the Board of Education of Topeka, Kansas,* but she certainly applauded the court's decision. With this decision, the long tradition of separate schools for black and white Americans was ended. Yet it was only the beginning of a long, hard struggle for greater equality that still continues.

Mary Terrell's part in the struggle would soon be overshadowed by more famous activists, including the Reverend Martin Luther King Jr. and Malcolm X. But her actions live on in every eating place in Washington, D.C. And her words still give courage to those who want to act but are afraid. "Keep on going," she wrote, "keep on insisting—keep on fighting injustice."

# Bibliography

## Books and Articles

Church, Roberta and Roland Walter. *Nineteenth Century Memphis Families of Color, 1850–1900.* Memphis, Tenn.: Burkes Bookstore, 1987.

Jones, Beverly Washington. *Quest for Equality: The Life and Writings of Mary Eliza Church Terrell, 1863–1954.* Brooklyn: Carlson Publishing Inc., 1990.

Salem, Dorothy C., ed. *African American Women: A Biographical Dictionary.* New York: Garland, 1993.

Shepperd, Gladys Byram. *Mary Church Terrell: Respectable Person.* Baltimore: Human Relations Press, 1959.

Smith, Jessie Carney, ed. *Epic Lives: One Hundred Black Women Who Made a Difference.* Detroit: Visible Ink Press, 1993.

Sterling, Dorothy. *Black Foremothers: Three Lives.* 2d ed. New York: The Feminist Press, 1988.

Terrell, Mary Church. *A Colored Woman in a White World.* 1940. Reprint, New York: Arno Press, 1980.

Terrell, Mary Church. "The Mission of Meddlers." *Voice of the Negro.* (Aug. 1905): 566–568.

Terrell, Mary Church. "What It Means to Be Colored in the Capital of the United States." In *Black Women in White America: A Documentary History,* edited by Gerda Lerner. New York: Vintage Books, 1973.

# Websites

<http://rs6.loc.gov/ammem/aap/terrell.html>
Part of *The Progress of a People,* a collection of information, photos, and pamphlets from the Library of Congress, this page includes a short biography of Mary Church Terrell and a link to a Real Audio version of one of Terrell's speeches, performed by an actor.

<http://www.tnstate.edu/library/digital/digitizing.html>
*Profiles of African Americans in Tennessee,* a collection of biographical sketches and photographs of prominent black Tennesseans, includes pages on Mary Church Terrell; her father, Robert Reed Church, Senior; and her half-brother, Robert Reed Church, Junior. An introductory essay by Bobby L. Lovett considers the history of African Americans in the state.

# Index

M Street High School, 27, 31
Malcolm X, 59
Model School, the, 19
Moss, Tom, 34, 48
Murphy's Department Store, 50

National Association of Colored
  Women (NACW), 38, 40, 42

Oberlin College, 24, 25

Phyllis Wheatley Home for
  Girls, 40

Scull, David, 48
segregation, 18–19, 33, 36, 57
slavery, 9–12, 14, 16, 27
Supreme Court, 54, 55, 57

Terrell, Mary Church (Mollie),
  birth of, 9; and board of
  education, 35, 36, 37, 42; and
  civil rights protests, 47, 48,
  50, 51, 52, 54, 55, 56, 59;
  death of, 57; education of,
  18, 19, 20, 21, 22, 23–24, 25,
  30, 31; as lecturer, 36–37, 38,
  42; and marriage, 24, 25, 29,
  30, 31; as mother, 33, 34, 35,
  40, 43, 44; as president of
  NACW, 38, 40, 42; and
  teaching, 26, 27, 30, 31, 35,
  37; as wife, 33, 41, 42, 44; as
  writer, 42, 44

Terrell, Phyllis (daughter), 40,
  44
Terrell, Robert Heberton
  (husband), 27, 33, 36; career
  of, 41; death of, 44;
  relationship with Mary, 29,
  30, 31
Thompson, Essie, 48
Thompson's Restaurant, 47, 48,
  51, 52, 54
Todd, Tomlinson, 45

Union House Hotel, 19

Wheatley, Phillis, 40
Wilberforce University, 26
Wright, Anna, 26

63

# About the Author

When **Gwenyth Swain** first heard about Mary Church Terrell, she remembers thinking what an unusual and interesting life Terrell had. From Terrell's teenage years as the only black student in her high school classes in Ohio to her struggle—while in her eighties—to desegregate eating places in Washington, D.C., her life was so inspiring that Ms. Swain had to tell others about it.

A writer and editor, Ms. Swain lives in St. Paul, Minnesota, with her husband and daughter. *Civil Rights Pioneer* is her ninth book for children. She is also the author of *The Road to Seneca Falls: A Story about Elizabeth Cady Stanton,* the biography of a women's rights pioneer.

# About the Illustrator

**Ellen Beier** has been drawing since she was a child living in New York. "I especially enjoy illustrating stories about people who lived in earlier times," says Ms. Beier. "In the case of Mary Church Terrell . . . her impact on history made this story particularly important to me."

Ms. Beier received her degree in art at the California College of Arts and Crafts. Later, while living overseas, she studied the work of great artists firsthand in the museums of Europe. She has illustrated many children's books, including several other biographies. She lives with her husband and son in Oregon.